CHRISTIAN CONCEPTS FOR GROWTH AND DEVELOPMENT

PRAYER & BIBLE BAND TOPICS

FALL QUARTER 2024
SEPTEMBER • OCTOBER • NOVEMBER

LARGE PRINT

Church Of God In Christ, INC.
PRAYER & BIBLE BAND TOPICS
FALL QUARTER 2024 | SEPTEMBER • OCTOBER • NOVEMBER

Bishop J. Drew Sheard
Presiding Bishop

Bishop Uleses C. Henderson, Jr.
Chairman, Publishing Board

Copyright © 2024 by Church Of God In Christ, Inc. Publishing House

Unless otherwise indicated, all Scripture references are taken from the authorized King James Version of the Bible.

Scripture quotations marked AMP are taken from the Amplified® Bible, Copyright © 1954, 1958, 1962, 1964, 1965, 1987 by The Lockman Foundation. Used by permission. All rights reserved.

Scripture quotations marked ESV® are taken from The Holy Bible, English Standard Version®, Copyright © 2001 by Crossway, a publishing ministry of Good News Publishers. Used by permission. All rights reserved.

Scripture quotations marked NASB are taken from the New American Standard Bible®, Copyright © 1960, 1962, 1963, 1968, 1971, 1972, 1973, 1975, 1977, 1995 by The Lockman Foundation. Used by permission. All rights reserved.

Scripture quotations marked NIV are taken from the HOLY BIBLE, NEW INTERNATIONAL VERSION®. Copyright © 1973, 1978, 1984 Biblica. Used by permission of Zondervan. All rights reserved.

Scripture quotations marked NLT are taken from the Holy Bible, New Living Translation, Copyright © 1996, 2004, 2007 by Tyndale House Foundation. Used by permission of Tyndale House Publishers, Inc., Carol Stream, Illinois 60188. All rights reserved.

Scripture quotations marked NKJV® are taken from the New King James Version®. Copyright © 1982 by Thomas Nelson, Inc. Used by permission. All rights reserved.

Scripture quotations marked NRSV are taken from the New Revised Standard Version Bible, Copyright © 1989, Division of Christian Education of the National Council of the Churches of Christ in the United States of America. Used by permission. All rights reserved.

Scripture quotations marked RSV are taken from the Revised Standard Version of the Bible, Copyright © 1952 [2nd edition, 1971] by the Division of Christian Education of the National Council of the Churches of Christ in the United States of America. Used by permission. All rights reserved.

Scripture quotations marked TLB are taken from The Living Bible®, 715800037417 Copyright © 1971, 1997 Tyndale House Foundation. Used by permission of Tyndale House Publishers, Inc., Carol Stream, Illinois 60188. All rights reserved.

Key Terms taken from the following:
www.thefreedictionary.com
www.merriam-webster.com
www.dictionary.reference.com

All rights reserved. No part of this publication may be reproduced, stored in a retrieval system or transmitted in any form or by any means—electronic, mechanical, photocopy, recording, or otherwise—without prior written permission of the copyright owners.

PAPERBACK: ISBN-13:978-1-68087-353-5   ISBN-10:1-68087-353-9
PAPERBACK LP: ISBN-13:978-1-68087-355-9   ISBN-10:1-68087-355-5

The Prayer & Bible Band Topics is published quarterly by
The Church Of God In Christ Publishing House
806 E. Brooks Rd • Memphis, TN 38116

Table Of Contents

4		Presiding Bishop's Letter
5		Preface
6	Lesson 1	Growing In Grace
9	Lesson 2	Learning To Praise God In And Through Everything
12	Lesson 3	Learning To Be Content
15	Lesson 4	The Second Birth
18	Lesson 5	Expectations About Heaven
21	Lesson 6	Power To Receive Good Things From God
24	Lesson 7	Love That Waxes Cold
27	Lesson 8	The Benefits Of Having Joy
30	Lesson 9	Courage To Deal With Limitations
33	Lesson 10	The Story Of The Good Samaritan
36	Lesson 11	God's Presence And Purpose In Your Life
39	Lesson 12	Learning To Increase Joy
42	Lesson 13	Joy Killers

Contributing Writers
Mother Lee VanZandt

THE GUIDE FOR WEEKLY BIBLE BAND MEETINGS

For weekly Bible Band meetings, the President should plan each meeting one week in advance.

- Secure a leader for devotion who will make preparations.
- Meetings should never last longer than two hours; however, let the Spirit of God lead.
- Appoint a different spiritually-minded individual for the leader of the devotional service.

ORDER OF SERVICE

- Call to Order (by the President)
- Singing
- Prayer

SCRIPTURE DEVOTIONAL READING

- A Five Minute Talk (on the devotion by the leader)
- President's Remarks
- President presents the teacher
- Announcements and Remarks
- Singing
- Benediction

LETTER from the PRESIDING BISHOP

Dear Saints of God,

Greetings in the Name of our Lord and Savior, Jesus Christ.

As we plan to embark upon a new year, I admonish each of you to take the time to reflect on God's goodness and ask Him to strengthen your hands for the work to be done. Our theme for 2024 is: "We Have Work to Do," John 9:4.

The Chairman of our Publishing Board, Bishop Uleses Henderson, Jr., and the members of that Board have been charged with preparing a curriculum that will challenge your faith and empower you to move forward in the work of the Lord.

I ask that you pray for our church, the leaders, and the congregants of this Grand Ole Church Of God In Christ.

In Ministry,

J. Drew Sheard,
Presiding Bishop & Chief Apostle
Church Of God In Christ, Inc.

PREFACE

Greetings to the Saints of God. I am so grateful to be able to greet you one more time. God has been mindful of us and allowed us to be on his wake-up list one more time. Millions didn't make it, but we were one of the ones who did.

God has brought many of us through sickness and afflictions, and we're still standing on his promises. We have experienced some losses, but he has kept us with peace and joy in our hearts.

This quarter, once again, we follow the leading of the Lord as we study His Word. His Word is absolutely a lamp unto our feet and a light unto our pathway. The more we study God's Word, the better we become equipped to share his word with someone else. For we are not ashamed of the gospel of Jesus Christ, for it is the power of God unto salvation to everyone who believes and receives it. So, we study to observe all things, whatever God desires for us.

Again, I thank my leaders, Presiding Bishop J. Drew Sheard, the General Board, our General Supervisor, Mother Barbara McCoo Lewis, and my brothers and sisters who support our great Church by buying and supporting our Publishing House.

Dr. Lee E. Van Zandt, Supervisor
Maryland Eastern Shore Ecclesiastical Department of Women
Chaplain, International Department of Women Executive Board
Elect Lady, COGIC World Mission Department
Contributing Editor, *Bible Band Topics*

Lesson 1 • First Week

GROWING IN GRACE

Background Reading
Malachi 4:2; 1 Corinthians 15:10; 2 Timothy 1:8-10; 2 Peter 1:2; Ephesians 4:29

Devotional Reading
Ephesians 4:8-16

Central Verse

"But grow in grace and in the knowledge of our Lord and Savior Jesus Christ. To Him be glory both now and forever. Amen."
2 Peter 3:18, KJV

" Rather, you must grow in the grace and knowledge of our Lord and Savior Jesus Christ."
2 Peter 3:18, NLT

Key Terms

Grow—To spring up and develop to maturity.
Grace—Unmerited divine assistance given to humans for their regeneration or sanctification: help given to people by God in overcoming temptation: a state of freedom from sin enjoyed through divine grace.
Mercy—Compassion or forbearance shown especially to an offender or one subject to one's power: kind and gentle treatment of someone (as a wrongdoer or opponent) having no right to it: a blessing as an act of divine love.

Introduction

The dictionary says that grace as a noun means simple elegance, refinement of movement, or courteous goodwill. As a verb, it means to do honor or credit to (someone or something) by one's presence. But when the believer talks about God's grace, he speaks from the standpoint of Christian theology. Grace is the "love and mercy given to us by God because He desires us to have it, not necessarily because of anything we have done to earn it." It is not a created substance of any kind. It is an attribute of God that is most manifest in the salvation of sinners. Except Father God draws men, they cannot be saved. For grace is the unmerited favor of God. The believer cannot work for it, for he cannot do enough to gain grace; it is freely given by God.

We used to sing a song that said, "Grace woke me up this morning; Grace started me on my way," Simply letting us know that we needed the grace of God to help us on our way for the day.

Lesson 1 • First Week

Discussion

Everything that has life should grow, including plants, animals, and humans. When there is no growth, it means that something is wrong. So, it is with the spirit man. Once a person accepts Jesus as his personal Savior, his life should show some growth. As newborn babies, there is a desire for the sincere milk of the word so they may grow.

To grow in grace means to mature as Christians, for God's grace makes it possible for a believer to live godly. God's grace makes it possible for the believer to cease making excuses for his behavior and his sins, and it enables him to lay aside his sins and become willing to live a sanctified life. If a believer becomes willing to sin no more, he becomes eligible for mercy instead of condemnation, for it is God's grace and mercy that allows the believer to be pardoned for his sins. When he repents, accepts the sacrifice of Jesus Christ, becomes baptized, and receives the gift of the Holy Ghost and the promise of eternal life.

"For by grace you have been saved through faith, and not of yourselves; it is the gift of God, not of works, lest anyone should boast." (Ephesians 2:8-9). Eternal life comes as a result of God's grace and mercy. It is something that you did not earn and did not deserve. It is a precious gift that only God can give to a believer. The believer cannot earn enough money to pay for this gift; it is not sold in any stores or venues.

In the Old Testament, God revealed Himself as a God of grace and mercy, who manifested love to His people not because they deserved it but because of His desire to be faithful to the promises made to Abraham, Isaac, and Jacob. Grace in the New Testament continues the theme of God's presence and love to the believers through Jesus Christ. The Holy Ghost gives the believer grace, which provides them with mercy, forgiveness, the desire, and the power to do God's will. God tells the believer that he can come boldly to His throne and, in the time of need, receive the grace he needs. Everything the believer does in the family of God is because of His grace.

God gives the unbelievers a measure of grace so that they may be able to believe on the Lord Jesus Christ and become followers of Him. God gives grace to the believer so that he may be made free from sin (Romans 6:20, 22). Also, so that he may be able to do His will for His good pleasure. Obedience is a gift of God's grace, for this flesh of mankind is an enemy against God, and on its own, it cannot and will not obey God nor His Word.

God gives the believer the Spirit of grace so that he can pray in some situations (Zechariah 12:10). It is because of grace that believers can witness to unbelievers and to proclaim God's goodness.

Conclusion

When someone has always worked for the things they wanted or needed, it is exceedingly difficult for them to adjust to someone giving them something, just because they love them. That is the way it is with the believer; he thinks that there must be something that he must do to receive the favor of God. That is why he must grow in grace and receive God's Word into his heart and spirit. As he gets more of God's Word and God's Spirit, his understanding increases, and his comprehension expands. He gets to the place where he can accept the pure love of God. Peter encouraged believers not to be led away by the wicked because of their lack of faith and understanding of the things of God. He urged them to seek to know their Lord and Savior, Jesus Christ. The early believers had accepted a doctrine that was different from the laws and actions of the old religious orders. Therefore, Paul encouraged them to

Lesson 1 • First Week

get as much knowledge as they could about the Savior Jesus Christ, whom they had embraced. The more they knew about Him, the better they could live and witness Him.

Sometimes, our understanding may be distorted when it comes to theology, politics, church, denominations, our faith, and other things that we have opinions about. But we must learn to rely on the Word of God and allow the Word to be our guide. As a follower of Christ, we must learn to think and live in the knowledge of God's amazing grace.

Questions

1. Why was it so hard for the believers to accept and understand the grace of God?
2. Why did God offer them His grace and mercy?
3. What are some of the ways of receiving God's grace and mercy?
4. Why does grace make every believer a winner in all situations?

_____
_____
_____
_____
_____

Essential Thought

God's grace makes the believer a winner every day through every situation.

Lesson 2 • Second Week

LEARNING TO PRAISE GOD IN AND THROUGH EVERYTHING

Background Reading
Psalm 34:1; 1 Thessalonians 2:13; 5:14-23; Ephesians 1:15-16; 1 Peter 2:9

Devotional Reading
2 Chronicles 20:15-25

Central Verse

"Praise ye the LORD: For it is good to sing praises unto God, For it is pleasant: and praise is comely." **Psalm 147:1, KJV**

"Praise the Lord! How good to sing praises to our God! How delightful and how fitting." **Psalm 147:1, NLT**

Key Terms

Jubilant—Feeling or expressing great joy.
Graditude—The state of being grateful (appreciative of benefits received).
Dimension—The range over which or the degree to which something extends: a level of existence or consciousness.

Introduction

The believer has been instructed to give God active praises for whatever is going on in his life. But for him to accomplish that, his trust must be in his God. This trust is a confident obedience to God's Word in all circumstances. The believer must learn to take God at His Word and live accordingly. If God said it, believe it, for it is so and so it is.

To receive the real essence of praises, the believer must consider the book of Psalms, a collection of psalms and songs written over 1,000 years ago. This book contains jubilant praises and sorrowful laments. The book is a testimony of God's loyal love towards His people in every circumstance. It is a book of Old Testament worship, and every psalm shows the anticipation of the culmination of God's praise in the death and the resurrection of His Son, Jesus Christ.

Praise gives the believer the sounds of Judah as he declares the praises of the God who brought them out of darkness through every challenge and every battle. There is a provision in Christ for everything that ails

Lesson 2 • Second Week

the believer. And when he learns to praise God in and for every mountain, every plateau, and every valley, he will find rest, peace, joy, and healing in the presence of a loving God.

Discussion

Sometimes, because of circumstances around a believer, he misses the benefit of praising God and being thankful to God for what is going on in his life. When he chooses to rejoice, meditate, and pray about things. Then, celebrate the fact that God has left him here on earth to experience suffering and hardships. He finds that God will allow him to arrive at a place where he cannot be broken even when he is overpowered because of the praise in his heart.

Prayer, praise, and thanksgiving are powers that transform everything and lead a believer into a greater dimension of faith and intimacy with God. When the believer asks, receives, and thanks, he becomes a disciple moving forward. The more thankful he becomes, he can look through the eyes of faith and see a brighter future.

Sometimes, believers forget they have a special reason to praise and be thankful. Believers are the recipients of the greatest gift in the world: forgiveness through Jesus Christ. Knowing how much Jesus loves them should encourage them to give thanks everyday through the good and the bad. As the believer praises God in and through everything, relief comes into his soul. He begins to recover lost faith and hope in his God. He reconnects to God's love for His world, he begins to understand God's profound love for humanity, and then he can love his neighbor as he loves himself.

Each believer should try to live a life of gratitude, just thinking about how good God is to him. Gratitude and thankfulness are not limited to emotions one experiences from time to time but are choices a believer must make. They are gifts that the believers can give back to God and His people. Having an attitude of gratitude means that a believer will decide not to complain but decides to shift their perspective and fill his life with praises and thanks to God.

It is easy to accept the temptation to grumble and complain about frustrations and disappointments, for life is filled with them. But the believer must make the decision to give thanks as he gives recognition to God for the gift of His dear Son and so many other wonderful benefits that He gives to each of us. If the believer would spend his time immersing himself in the Bible verses that encourage him why and how he can give thanks, he won't settle for the ploys the enemies bring to cause him to be discontent and spend his time grumbling and complaining.

Conclusion

The story of Jehoshaphat and Israel is the story of many believers. As the enemies of Ammon, Mt. Seir, and Moab approached them, Jehoshaphat, the leader, was afraid, but he knew he could not defeat these armies. So, he turned to God, enlisted God's help, and instructed the people about what to do. He proclaimed a fast throughout the entire land. He required all the people to fast and pray. Some things happen and are happening in our lives; we cannot do anything to stop them from happening. The believer must do as Jehoshaphat did, realize that the battle is not his, but if he can praise God, God will do the rest. The believer doesn't always have to be doing something to win the battle. Sometimes, he needs to stand still and see the salvation or deliverance of the Lord.

Lesson 2 • Second Week

Amid what could have been a fierce battle, Jehoshaphat appointed singers and told them what to say. They began to give praise and thanksgiving to God on the battlefield, and He went to work for them. King David said, "I will bless the Lord at all times, and His praises shall be in my mouth, not cursing, defeat, negative words, but praises. He knew that God inhabits the praises of His people.

So, as the believers grow in God, they must learn to be thankful at all times and give God the sacrifice of praise, which is the fruit of their lips.

Questions

1. What is so powerful about a believer praising God?
2. When should he give God praise?
3. Why should he give God praise?
4. What are the benefits to the believer when he gives God praise?
5. How can the believer compare himself to Jehoshaphat?

Essential Thought

Praising God is what believers do because it is in their DNA.

Lesson 3 • Third Week

LEARNING TO BE CONTENT

Background Reading
Job 6:28; Ecclesiastes 4:6; Philippians 4:11; Hebrews 13:5; 1 Timothy 6:8

Devotional Reading
2 Kings 6:1-7

Central Verse

"But godliness with contentment is great gain."   1 Timothy 6:6, KJV

"Yet true godliness with contentment is itself great wealth."   1 Timothy 6:6, NLT

Key Terms

Content—To make happy: pleased and satisfied with what one has or is.
Discontent—Lack of satisfaction with one's possessions, status, or situation: lack of contentment.

Introduction

To be content means that a person is in a state of satisfaction or in a state of peaceful happiness. In this day when so many people are living better than they have ever lived, there are only a few people who seem to be content with their lives. The spirit of dissatisfaction is everywhere, for it seems that the more a person gets, the more he wants. Many are like the farmer whose barns were full and he decided to tear them down and build bigger barns. He was not content to just have his barns full and be happy to give the overflow to someone else who was in need. Instead, he decided to increase the capacity of his barns. People would probably live longer, have less stress, less pressure problems and have an altogether healthier life, if they became content with what they already have.

Discussion

Contentment as well as discontentment is a learned behavior. Just as a person learns it, they can turn around and unlearn it as fast as they learned it.

Being content gives the believer a better outlook on life. Psychology Today, April 2021 says, "the greatest wealth that a person can possess is contentment, not money." Many people seem to think that if they had all the money they needed, it would make them happy and content. But according to Psychology Today, this means "that being content wherever we are with our lives is more valuable than being wealthy."

Lesson 3 • Third Week

When a person is content with his life, it means that he is satisfied with what he has and with who he is. It means that he does not compare himself to others nor does he wish that he had a different life. He will feel that he is living a life that he is satisfied with, and he is willing to accept himself for who he is. Contentment means that a person does not spend valuable time wishing that he could be someone else. But he values who he is and tries to better himself without being frustrated or stressed out.

Contentment is a very necessary virtue when you are living for Jesus. For contentment assures the believer of inner peace and allows him to be able to show love and gratitude to others as the Lord would have him do. It also helps a believer to know his purpose in the body of Christ. This causes him to be steadfast in his commitment to the cause of Christ. The word of the Lord tells the believer that a double minded man is unstable in all his ways. Discontent allows the enemy the freedom to attack the believers' mind and causes him to become double minded. When a person is double minded, their words nor actions can be counted on to be dependable. The word of the Lord tells the believer that contentment gives the believer great gain, it is very profitable. Contentment comes from our relationship to what is in a person, rather than their reaction to their surroundings. When there is contentment, anger, sadness, joy, frustration, money, challenges, nor excitement can define a believer.

When a believer is content, he has the key to happiness. He may be ambitious, but he is never greedy. He can sit back, relax and be grateful for all that he has achieved. He will have peace of mind. The word of the Lord admonishes the believer to seek peace, even to pursue peace. As much as he can learn to be at peace with his fellow believers, he can also, learn to be content.

Contentment will help a believer be incredibly positive about himself and this will help him to facilitate growth and self-improvement in his life. In his quest for self-improvement, the believer must be able to see the signs of God's provision. Either through His word or from life learned lessons. In his search he will not be anxious but will be filled with peace as he reminds himself that God is listening to and sees his needs.

A contented person understands that God designed him to achieve wonderful things, and that he is unique in his personality, his abilities, and his relationship with God and people. He knows that no one else on this earth can be him, live his life and accomplish what God has for him. So, contentment helps him to focus on the things that matter in his life. He no longer desires the green grass on the other side of the fence.

Situations will come into everyone's life at one time or another, but a contented person will not become unhappy nor dissatisfied when those times come. He will be able to settle his spirit and realize that God is yet in control in his life, and whatever is going on is absolutely working for his good. He knows that God is bigger than anything that he could ever face. A believer learns how to be content in his circumstances even when he is not content with them. Paul said in Philippians 4:11, "Not that I am speaking of being in need, for I have learned in whatever situation I am in to be content."

Conclusion

We are certainly living in the last days, just as Paul told the believers that it would be perilous times. Which is why many of the older Saints long for that time for years gone by. Many of them have sad

Lesson 3 • Third Week

hearts and find themselves complaining. But when life around them is turning into a whirlwind of confusion, and they wish that things will end. They need to remember that Jesus has brought into the believer's heart with Himself, everything they need. The believer must lift his eyes up and know that his redemption draws nigh, knowing that having Jesus in his life, as the head of his life, brings true contentment. So, while living in the midst of a fast-paced, consumer-driven society, pray that God will help to give complete contentment.

Questions

1. Why is contentment so important in the life of a believer?
2. What are the negative points for a believer if he is dscontent?
3. What can a believer do to gain contentment in his life?
4. How can God help the belever become content?

_____
_____
_____
_____
_____
_____

Essential Thought

Learning to be content in a situation while you are not content with the situation is great gain.

Lesson 4 • Fourth Week

THE SECOND BIRTH

Background Reading
Psalm 51:5; Lamentations 5:7; 1 John 3:9; 1 Peter 1:23; Titus 3:5

Devotional Reading
John 3:1-12

Central Verse

"Jesus answered and said unto him, verily, verily, I say unto thee, except a man be born again, he cannot see the Kingdom of God."
John 3:3, KJV

"Jesus replied, "I tell you the truth, unless you are born again, you cannot see the Kingdom of God."
John 3:3, NLT

Key Terms

Miscarriage—Spontaneous expulsion of a human fetus before it is viable and especially between the 12th and 28th weeks of gestation.
Abortion—The termination of a pregnancy after, accompanied by, resulting in, or closely followed by the death of the embryo or fetus: failure of a project or action to reach full development.
Regeneration—Spiritual renewal or revival: an act or the process of being formed or created again : the state of being regenerated.
New Birth—To be born again, or to experience the new birth, is a phrase, particularly in evangelicalism and Pentecostalism, that refers to a "spiritual rebirth," or a regeneration of the human spirit.

Introduction

One of the greatest miracles of all time is the miracle of a baby being born. It takes the participation of two persons, a man who has sperms and a woman who has eggs, to come together and the sperm must connect with the egg to start the journey of a baby being born. The process must go from start to finish, for the baby to come forth. Many times, the sperm has connected with an egg, but never materialized into a baby being born. Sometimes there is a natural interruption, called miscarriage, which happens for various reasons, and sometimes interruption occurs because it is a planned interruption called abortion. How ever the interruption comes, it puts an end to the life cycle to what would have or could have been a baby.

There is a natural and then a spiritual. Just as there are interruptions in the natural, there can be interruptions in the spiritual. Just as an interruption can come in the natural and stop the cycle of the birth of a child, it can happen in the spiritual. The spiritual life can be stopped by ungodly choices and unrighteous living, and death comes spiritually. Romans eight and thirteen tells the believer that if he is being led by the flesh, he will die. Sin and the refusal to follow the Holy Spirit will cause death to the new birth of a believer and will exclude him from entering into the kingdom of God.

Lesson 4 • Fourth Week

Discussion

One of the most fundamental doctrines of the Christian faith is regeneration or the spiritual birth or the new birth. Without the new birth, one cannot see the kingdom of God, receive eternal life or receive salvation through Jesus Christ. All humans are born in sin because of the sin of Adam and his wife Eve. By one man sin entered the world, and death by sin, and so death passed upon all men, for that all have sinned: (Romans 5:12). And by one man's death humanity can be freed from the curse of a broken law, by the man Jesus Christ.

After the curse was put upon mankind, nothing could change it but the shedding of Jesus' blood, otherwise there was no remission for sin. Then if a man wanted to be in right standing with God, he had to be born again, or he must receive the New Birth, because on his own, he could not obey nor please God.

The New Birth is the spiritual rebirth of every person who surrenders their life and their will to Jesus Christ. He places his faith, his hope and trust in Jesus and becomes spiritually reborn. "The old has passed away; behold the new has come". (2 Corinthians 5:17).

Regeneration is a re-creating and transformation of the believer by God and The Holy Spirit. The believer must not conform to the world's system, but he must be transformed by the renewing of his mind. He must allow the process of eternal life from God Himself to be imparted to his life, and he becomes a child of God, and a new person (2 Corinthians 5:17; Colossians 3:9-10). With the new birth, the believer is now created after God "in righteousness and true holiness" (Ephesians 4:24).

Regeneration comes to the believer only after he repents of his sin, turn to God and place his personal faith in Jesus Christ as his Lord and as his Savior. Without faith, it is impossible to please God, so his faith must line up with his actions.

The believer who is really born again is set free from the bondage of sin and receives a spiritual desire and disposition to obey and follow the leading of the Holy Spirit. There are four things that will let someone know that a person is born again, the born- again believer, will live a righteous life, he will love other believers, avoid a life of sin and he will not love the world. (1 John 2:15-16). These are some of the reasons Jesus told Nicodemus, that if he wanted to see the kingdom of God, he must be born again.

To remain a child of God without a sincere desire to please God can only be accomplished through the grace given to the believer by Jesus Christ.

Conclusion

Nicodemus understood how a baby could be born out of his mother's womb, but he could not understand how he could go back into the womb and be born a second time. Jesus told him that except a man be born of water and of the Spirit, he cannot enter into the kingdom of God. Jesus was referring to the cleansing work of the Holy Spirit in the new birth. In Titus three and five, Paul speaks of the "washing of regeneration, and renewing of the Holy Ghost."

Jesus explained that you cannot see the wind, but it's activity and it's sound identifies it, so it is with the new birth. It's identified by its activities and its sound.

Lesson 4 • Fourth Week

The believer must understand as Jesus said to Nicodemus that the flesh cannot understand the things of the Spirit, and the things of the Spirit will not understand nor accept the things of the flesh.

The believer's life in God's family is based on a conditional act, based on his faith in Christ Jesus throughout his earthly existence. He must have a life of sincere obedience and love to God and the things of God and His kingdom.

Questions

1. What is the new birth that Jesus talked about to Nicodemus?
2. How can a person receive this new birth?
3. Why is it necessary for the believer to be born again?
4. What is the Holy Spirit's role in the new birth?

_____
_____
_____
_____
_____
_____

Essential Thought

Those who live in immorality and follow the world's ways demostrate that they are yet unregenerated and are the children of satan.

Lesson 5 • Fifth Week

EXPECTATIONS ABOUT HEAVEN

Background Reading
Job 11:8; Psalm 8:3; 19:1; Isaiah 66:22; Hosea 2:21; Luke 21:25-28; Acts 7:49; Revelations 4:8-11

Devotional Reading
Revelations 21:1-27

Central Verse

"But lay up for yourselves treasures in heaven, where neither moth nor rust doth corrupt, and where thieves do not break through to steal."
Matthew 6:20, KJV

"Store your treasures in heaven, where moths and rust cannot destroy, and thieves do not break in and steal." **Matthew 6:20, NLT**

Key Terms

Heaven—The expanse of space that seems to be over the earth like a dome: the vault or arch of the sky.

Biblical definition of Heaven—It is primarily God's dwelling place in the biblical tradition: a parallel realm where everything operates according to God's will.

Introduction

Most of the people who were raised in Christian homes were told about going to Heaven. It was said to be the most beautiful, wonderful, and amazing place that anyone could ever want to go to. It was said to be more beautiful than anyplace on earth. God knows there are places on this earth that are breath-takingly beautiful. But heaven is reported to be more gorgeous than any place a person can find.

After growing up hearing about how Jesus who died in our place and rose again from the dead to guarantee our resurrection to such a place. It gives the believers the incentive to want to go there, knowing that heaven will be their home. The expectation of seeing the Glory of God in heaven motivates the believer to look forward to going to heaven one day. This belief has given the believers a new home and a new hope. This causes him to live every day for heaven, dropping the cares and weights of this world. Knowing that they are just for a season, but they will pass away. Jesus said in the book of John chapter fourteen and two, that He was going away to prepare a place for the believers, for in His Father's house there are many mansions.

Lesson 5 • Fifth Week

Discussion

Heaven is a wonderful place where the believers expect to go and spend eternity there with God, Jesus, the Holy Spirit, the Angels, and all the Saints from the ages gone by. Jesus lets the believers know that the way to heaven is small and narrow and only a few people will find it (Matthew 7:14).

The believers have much to look forward to when they get to eternity, for none but the pure in heart, shall see God. The believers have been told about the fabulous jewels in heaven, streets of gold, gates of pearls. The New Jerusalem reflecting the glory of God which reflects the lights like unto precious stones, like a jasper stone, clear as crystal, a great wall that has twelve gates. The city has twelve foundations, # 1 jasper, #2 sapphire, # 3 a chalcedony, # 4 an emerald; #5 sardonyx, # 6 sardius, # 7 chrysolite; # 8 beryl; # 9, a topaz; # 10 a chrysoprasus; # 11 jacinth, #12 an amethyst. There is a river there, many trees, and one tree has leaves that are good for the healing of the nations.

It has always been the desire of the Saints to look forward to going home to live with Jesus. Jesus came to the world as a baby, but always let the believers know that one day He was going back home to His father's house. The older Saint's sang, "If you live right, heaven belonged to you." Heaven is where Jesus is now preparing a place for the believers to live, because when they get to heaven, they will have new bodies without the curse of sin. There will be no one who is blind, deaf or lame in heaven according to Isaiah thirty-five verses five and six, and Philippians three and twenty-one.

The Bible says that "The Lord has established His throne in heaven, and His kingdom rules over all" (Psalm 103:19). The believer will be able to enjoy a new heaven and a new earth, for the Holy city, New Jerusalem, shall come down from heaven (Revelation 21:1-2). There shall be no more pain, no more death nor sorrow, for God shall wipe away all tears from the believer's eyes. According to Isaiah sixty-five and twenty-five there shall be perfect peace, for in heaven the wolf and the lamb shall eat together. The lion shall eat straw like the ox and the serpents food shall be dust, for Jesus the Prince of Peace shall be there. Wherever Jesus is the Spirit of Peace will be there.

Now when Jesus returns to the earth, every knee shall bow to Him, and every tongue shall confess to God (Romans 14:11). And when He comes in the clouds, every eye shall see Him (Revelation 1:7). But everyone will not go home with Him to spend eternity with Him. A believer cannot live good enough to go to heaven, for his righteousness is as filthy rags. It is by faith that the believer is saved, not by works, for salvation is a gift from God. The believer must believe and receive the Gospel of Jesus Christ. For there is only one way to heaven and Jesus paid for the right-of-way when He died the cruel death of being crucified on that rugged cross. The believer must believe and receive the fact that Jesus was born of a virgin, came from God the Father, took on flesh and lived on this earth as a man, and died on the cross for the sins of humanity. He was buried in a grave but rose out of the grave on the third morning, walked and talked with His disciples and then stepped on a cloud and descended back into heaven. Jesus is now at the right hand of His Father interceding for the believer.

There will be some believers who will come before God and tell Him all the wonderful things they did while here on earth. But God is going to dismiss them and let them know that their works were done out of His will, through their will and their own willfulness.

Lesson 5 • Fifth Week

Conclusion

Believers has been practicing for years, praising, and worshiping God, getting ready for the heavenly atmosphere of praise and worship. They expect to join with the angels singing and giving praise around the Throne of God. They have the expectation of practicing getting ready to sing, shout and dance when they see Jesus. Thanking Him for dying for them and making them free from the bondage of sin. They are preparing to go to wherever Jesus will be, because, wherever Jesus is, it is heaven.

Questions

1. Where is heaven?
2. How can you get to heaven?
3. Who lives in heaven?
4. What will you see in heaven?

_____
_____
_____
_____
_____
_____

Essential Thought

Heaven is a prepared place for a prepared people.

Lesson 6 • First Week

POWER TO RECEIVE GOOD THINGS FROM GOD

Background Reading
Deuteronomy 33:6; Psalm 84:11; Ecclesiastes 2:24; Luke 11:13; 12:32; Romans 8:28; 2 Corinthians 9:8; Titus 2:9-10;

Devotional Reading
Joshua 23:1-15

Central Verse

"Your iniquities have turned away these things, and your sins have witholden good things from you." **Jeremiah 5:25, KJV**

"Your wickedness has deprived you of these wonderful blessings. Your sin has robbed you of all these good things." **Jeremiah 5:25, NLT**

Key Terms

Iniquity—Gross injustice: a wicked act or thing.
Masterpiece—A work done with extraordinary skill: a supreme intellectual or artistic achievement.
Unique—Being the only one: being without a like or equal: able to be distinguished from all others of its class or type.

Introduction

A person raised in a Christian home has always been taught that God is his heavenly father and that He loves and cares about His children. Whatever concerns His children concerns Him. He tells His children to cast all their cares upon Him, for He cares about whatever it is that bothers His children. God says that if humans, who are basically evil (without God in their lives) know how to give good gifts, how much more does He know how to give good things to those who ask for them.

God knows what things His children have need of, but He wants His children to communicate with Him and ask Him for what they want. Some children have problems communicating with their heavenly Father because of the negative relationship they have had with their earthly Father. But he needs to learn and know that God is a righteous Father and He is good and perfect all the time.

Lesson 6 • First Week

Discussion

Sometimes it has been necessary for some people to experience negative things in their relationships in the natural family life to be able to appreciate and bring them to the good things that God has in store for them. Living in a society that is in love with self can sometimes cause a person to become unhappy and unfulfilled, because their focus has been primarily on themselves. Many times, they do not know or don't remember that they were not created for themselves. They don't remember or don't know that they were created to give glory to God. They are not aware that they have been chosen for a greater purpose than just being happy for the sake of being happy.

When a person becomes aware that his purpose includes living according to God's good pleasure and His will, it changes his entire perspective on his life. The believer has the privilege to just ask, seek, and knock and so many good things become available to him (Matthew 7:7-8). God is a loving compassionate God who desires to give every good and perfect gift to His children. But they must be aware of that and be positioned to receive the gifts that God has to offer. For He daily loads His children with benefits.

Jesus told His disciples to ask for His kingdom to come in their lives when they pray. He wants each believer to experience His kingdom, which is not meat nor drink, but it is joy and peace in the Holy Ghost. But the believers must be willing to deny themselves of some of their fleshly desires and walk in the fruit of the Spirit and increase their trust in their God. Only then can the believer enjoy and receive the Kingdom blessings while he lives here on earth.

As dear children, they must learn to know and become comfortable with their heavenly Father. As they develop a relationship with Him, they will become comfortable being in His arms. Realizing that they are safe in His arms because all fear is gone, only love, power, and soundness of mind remain. God wants His children to know that He is the father of the father-less, He is father to those who are directionless, for He is a God of Leadership, and wants to lead those who have no leader. He is a good God who wants to lead you in paths of righteousness as He leads your heart.

In a world that leaves believers sad, empty, burned-out, and isolated, God wants to lead you to purpose, significance, to connection, joy, and peace. He wants you to enjoy the abundant life that He so freely gives.

Conclusion

Every believer needs to know that God designed them to see Him, know His character, and let the truth of His goodness lead to a deeper relationship with Him. When a believer can see God for who He is his heart will become stirred to find rest in His goodness and love and seek to be like His wonderful character.

Remember that God did not make a mistake when He made you, you may be the result of what someone labeled "a mistake," but not so with God. He gave you your unique gifts that are a part of the calling that is on your life, and you must remember just how special you are. Really, you are God's masterpiece, and you need to walk and talk in God's goodness with a fresh energy from the Holy Spirit.

Lesson 6 • First Week

Questions

1. Why is it necessary to have power to receive certain things?
2. What are some of the good things that God does for his children?
3. Why is God so good to his children?

___

___

___

___

___

Essential Thought

Just ask for what you need and receive it.

Lesson 7 • Second Week

LOVE THAT WAXES COLD

Background Reading
Song Of Solomon 8:7; Matthew 24:11; Roman 5:8; 2 Corinthians 2:4; Ephesians 6:12-13; 1 Timothy 6:10; 1 John 4:7-21

Devotional Reading
Matthew 24:1-14

Central Verse

"And because iniquity shall abound, the love of many shall wax cold." Matthew 24:12, KJV

"Sin will be rampant everywhere; and the love of many will grow cold." Matthew 24:12, NLT

Key Terms

Wax cold—Is a biblical phrase used only in Matthew 24:12. The Greek word psugestetai from the root psucho means – to breathe cool by blowing, to grow cold. One scholar describes it as "spiritual energy blighted (spoiled/damaged) or chilled by a malign (evil) or poisonous wind."
Immoral—Not relating to principles of right and wrong in behavior: not agreeing with a standard of right behavior: morally bad.
Wickedness—The quality or state of being morally very bad: something morally reprehensible.
Abound—To be present in large numbers or in great quantity: to be prevalent.

Introduction

God is love, (1 John 4:8) He is the very essence of what love is all about. Love is so important in the life of a believer that Jesus said, "by love men would know that they are His disciples" (John 13:35). There are many signs that believers have, but none are as powerful as the sign of love. For the Word tells the believer that if he does not love, he does not know God. Love is the greatest gift that any believer can have, and it is so important in the growth of a ministry. Hal David and Burt Bacharach wrote a song that said, "What The World Needs Now Is Love Sweet Love," which has much truth in it. Jesus told His disciples that love is the greatest commandment. He told them that no one had any greater love than He did, because He laid down His life for His friends.

Discussion

There are some attributes of love that are necessary in the lives and growth of every believer. John tells the believer that they should love one another because love is of God. And everyone who does not love each other does not know God. Because of love God sent His only begotten Son into the world that believers might live through Him. God sent Jesus, not because we loved Him, but because

Lesson 7 • Second Week

He loved us. Because God loved us, we should love one another. When a believer has God in him, he has love in him. Many things are happening in our world that can cause a person to become fearful, but perfect love casts out fear.

As our world changes with the iniquity that is filling it, the believer must draw close to God and His Word. Jesus warned the believer that in the last days things would change, and the demonic activity would become more prevalent. He said that where iniquity or the violation of the law, wickedness, transgression of the law continues in our world, the love of Jesus Christ will be pushed further and further away from us. Until there will no longer be love and the fear of God in our world. Any and everything will become permissible.

We see the moral decline in our society everywhere in all the institutions that used to show reverence to God. There seems to be little tolerance and respect toward others. Most people are selfish and only live for themselves. Proverbs thirty tells the believers that there are generations that are rebellious against their parents, no respect for mothers and fathers, parents focused on themselves, their careers, and their happiness instead of on their children. This generation is drowning in isolation and starving for love and commitment. They are searching for something, but don't have a clue what it is. But the followers of Jesus know that it is end-time and the love of many has waxed cold or grown cold. But know that true love cannot become cold because it is sustained by Christ who is able to keep us from falling (Jude 1:24). But those without the power of the Holy Spirit will become colder and colder in the last days.

Remember the love of money is the root of all evil, (1 Timothy 6:10). The believers must be aware of the false prophets and the prosperity preachers who only talk about prospering financially and never talk about the soul prospering. Watch out for those who do everything from a self-love and selfish way, only me and mine. Never including the homeless, the oppressed, the poor and needy, the fatherless and orphans, the widows, and single mothers.

Conclusion

Today, it is being seen more than ever before. The news media is filled with wicked acts, laws being changed from righteous behavior to wicked agendas. Wickedness is increasing in governments and materializing in greed. The rich are becoming richer, and the poor are becoming poorer causing poverty rates to skyrocket, which allows crimes to increase. Yes, iniquity is abounding more and more. When Christ is not present, darkness increases and men love darkness because their deeds are evil.

The believers must stay prayerful and watchful. Churches are closing and people are feeding on negative news. The neighborhoods are becoming crime infested and mass shootings are taking place. Believers must not allow these dark times to negatively affect them and cause them to turn away from God and the body of believers. They must not allow their minds to become bitter and cold; they must stay mindful of Jesus's words and keep their light burning. They must continue to show love to everyone they meet, remembering that Jesus is their example. As He loves us, we love them.

It is important that believers refuse to seek glory for themselves, they must not get in the rat race for accolades and power. If they do, they will lose sight of their brother or sister and their love will flee from them by waxing cold. True love works no ill will to its neighbor, for true love will do everything that it can to promote his brother. It will bring glory to God, honor to Jesus and good to everybody that it comes in contact with.

Lesson 7 • Second Week

Questions

1. When iniquity abounds, how must the believers conduct themselves?
2. How can we set a good moral standard for the generations after us?
3. Why must the believers continue to be watchful and prayerful?
4. How can believers continue to show that Jesus is their example?

_____
_____
_____
_____
_____
_____

Essential Thought

Where sin and iniquity abounds, the grace of God doth much more abound.

Lesson 8 • Third Week

THE BENEFITS OF HAVING JOY

Background Reading
Psalm 21:1; 27:1; 35:27; 118:14; John 15:11; Galatians 5:22-23; 1 Thessalonians 2:19

Devotional Reading

Central Verse

"These things have I spoken unto you, that my joy might remain in you, and that your joy might remain in you, and that your joy might be full."
John 15:11, KJV

"I have told you these things so that you will be filled with joy, Yes, your joy will overflow!"
John 15:11, NLT

Key Terms

Despairing—Given to, arising from, or marked by despair: devoid of hope.
Overwhelmed—Overcome by force or numbers: completely overcome or overpowered by thought or feeling.
Benefit—Something that produces good or helpful results or effects or that promotes well-being: to be useful or profitable to.

Introduction

The joy of the Lord is strength! Each believer will encounter challenges as he lives for God. Today there are many things that will drain all the joy out of their lives if they did not have Jesus and the promise that He has given to them. Life could become very dreary without the light of the gospel in their lives. Therefore, it becomes necessary to have something that brings joy into their hearts. Sometimes the pressures of life weigh upon them until their hearts feel like fainting.

Sometimes the believer needs a spontaneous joy that comes unexpectedly at a time when he would have fainted if he had not seen the goodness of the Lord in the land of the living. But thank God for His joy that comes like a river, flooding the soul of the believer, giving strength when he feels so tired and weary.

Discussion

Joy is one of the fruits of the Spirit that is so necessary for the spiritual growth in the life of a believer, for in God's presence there is fullness of joy. Ephesians five and verse nine tells the believer that the fruit of the Spirit is in all goodness, righteousness, and truth. God displays His fruit in the believer when they give their lives to Him. When the believer becomes overwhelmed, he can reach out and get some joy.

Lesson 8 • Third Week

Jesus offers everlasting joy, despite the pain that comes in the night season of their lives, there is yet hope, because joy comes in the morning. In the morning the believer's ears, eyes and heart are more open. Peter tells the believers that God's ears are always open unto the righteous. God is intentional in His care for His people and God is always good.

There are times in a believer's life when he seems to lose direction, life throws some blows that are hard to handle. Sometimes the believer wonders if he will make it through the dilemma that he finds himself in.

But God will allow something or someone to come along and give him hope that will help him to obtain the tools that are needed to survive and see the joy in his situation. Life brings unexpected pain, sometimes causing the believer to question whether God is there or even cares about what is happening in their lives. The believer begins to wonder, can grief and sorrow coexist with joy? Well, know that God will allow true joy to grow in the soil of the believer's pain.

All believers' experience fear and anxiety in their lives, but they cannot allow fear and anxiety to keep them overwhelmed and unable to enjoy the life that God has for them. God's word helps them to focus on His promises and helps them to become anchored in their hearts when these waves of anxiety knock them around. That is when they must find more peace and joy and stand on the promises of God.

Many are the losses in life that cause a believer to stagger and feel like he just will not recover from them. That is when he remembers and relies on God's promises, knowing that God is not a man that He should lie. For every promise that He has made, He is able to, and will keep them. God will give the believer a praise or some joy for the spirit of heaviness. He will encourage the believer to stand tall on His word, because even in despairing times, God provides joy in mourning.

Unforgiveness is like a cancer to the soul and when it is left unchecked, refusing to forgive can be just as deadly to the believer's soul as physical disease is to the body. But God is able to help the believer to humble himself until he can find joy in forgiving his fellowman. For as he forgives others, he releases blessings upon himself. The believer becomes the winner, he's the one who can be joyous knowing that he is free. The Saints used to sing, "Oh the joy that came to me, when I knew that I was free, when my Savior found me and wrapped His loving arms around me, oh the joy that came to me."

Being free from unforgiveness gives the believer a sense of hope, direction, joy, and power. Because he is no longer bound and has no more chains of bondage holding him.

Forgiveness brings freedom to the believer from those who have hurt him. Forgiveness breaks the handcuffs and opens the door. It removes revenge, bitterness, and hatred from their soul. Forgiveness allows the believer to experience total freedom and allows the believer to learn to love others as Christ loves the Church. Then God will shower the believer with unspeakable joy and limitless freedom. For forgiveness is a powerful healing force.

Conclusion

During life's difficulties, joy can sometimes feel out of reach. But Jesus has more for His followers than a life of striving, pain, and discontent. He offers abundant life, life to the fullest, life brimming with joy. Sometimes the believer just has to remember that God's word will connect him with Jesus' joy through life's circumstances. It is up to the believer to embrace joy in Jesus' presence, for in His presence there

Lesson 8 • Third Week

is fullness of joy and life everlasting.

Whatever your personality or circumstances, God has a word of encouragement for you. For He wants the believers to know joy. God doesn't want the believer to just be happy, He wants every believer to experience joy, for they were meant to have joy. So, make that choice to fill your life with joy.

Questions

1. Where does joy come from?
2. How does joy help the believer?
3. What is God's role in your joy?
4. What does the believer have to do to maintain his joy?
5. What does strength have to do with joy?

_____
_____
_____
_____
_____
_____

Essential Thought

The joy that you have did not come from the world;
so, don't let the world take it away.

Lesson 9 • Fourth Week

COURAGE TO DEAL WITH LIMITATIONS

Background Reading
Numbers 11:23; 1 Kings 18:39; Proverbs 24:10; Ezekiel 34:30; Ephesians 3:20; Romans 8:14

Devotional Reading
Psalm 78:19-54

Central Verse

"Yea, they turned back and tempted God, and limited the Holy One of Israel."
Psalm 78:41, KJV

"Again and again they tested God's patience and provoked the Holy One of Israel."
Psalm 78:41, NLT

Key Terms

Mediocrity—The quality or state of being moderate or low quality, value, ability, or performance: ordinary.
Unlimited—Lacking any controls: having no boundaries.
Specific—Something peculiarly adapted to a purpose or use: restricted to a particular individual, situation, effect, or reaction.

Introduction

You were not created to live with limitations and it is time to fulfill your supernatural destiny by agreeing with what God says about you. Sometimes the believer has to challenge the boundaries that culture, circumstances, and beliefs has set on their God. So, they have to take the limits off of their faith and experience the limitless miraculous love of their untamable God. God wants every believer to live out his life in ways that defy the ordinary. Limitations keep a believer in a life of mediocrity. The believer must defy the limitations if they want to live a life of fulfilled potential.

Unlimited faith helps the believer to deepen his faith in God by learning how his trust in God can develop and grow. Unlimited faith challenges the believer to look to the cross, knowing that his sufficiency is not of himself, but of God.

Discussion

Our God is all-powerful, there is nothing that He cannot do. He can do exceedingly abundantly above all that we ask or think. Our God can do the impossible. For what is impossible to man, is possible with God. He is the God of all flesh and there is nothing too hard for God.

Lesson 9 • Fourth Week

The human part of the believer finds it quite easy to put limits on God. So many times, the believer puts God on a level with them, not realizing that God is not a man, He is a Spirit, He is the God of the Universe, He is the God who made everything. His Word tells the believer that the earth is the Lords (1 Corinthians 10:26), everything on this earth belongs to Him. He allows people to take ownership of what belongs to Him, but ultimately it still belongs to Him.

God was so good to Israel after they had been in slavery over four hundred years. He appointed a leader who led them out of Egypt, across a great sea, without a bridge. Led them to a land and told them to go in and possess that land. Because they were so used to putting limits on things, they convinced themselves that they couldn't do it. Because they put limits on God's ability, they had to spend forty years wandering in the wilderness. While they wandered God fed them with manna from heaven, sent quails into their camp, led them by fire at night and a cloud by day. God led them through a land that they had never been in before without a GPS. Their clothes and shoes never wore out and none of them were feeble or sick (Psalm 105:37), but yet, they foolishly limited God.

Many believers are like the children of Israel, they have had experiences with the awesome power of God. He has saved them, healed them, performed miracles for them by doing things that was impossible under normal circumstances, but many still limit what God can and will do for them. God has told the believers to trust and obey Him, ask, and believe Him (Matthew 7:7), but for whatever reason, they can't seem to obey Him. They live beneath their privileges because of the limits they put on God.

The song says, "oh what peace we often forfeit, oh what needless pains we bear, all because we do not carry, everything to God in prayer." Sometimes the believer takes his petition to God in prayer, but the prayer is limited because of the unbelief of the believer.

Time after time God sent His prophets to encourage the people to trust Him. He sent Ezekiel to let the people know that He was going to make some changes in the Government. In fact, He was going to allow the Government to be changed. He just needed His people to trust the process. He needed them to stop limiting Him. No matter what is going on in our countries, do not minimize God's power and do not limit Him.

Elijah stood against Ahab the prophets of Baal, He and God showed them what can happen when a man of God trusts the living God and puts no limits nor restraints on Him. God indeed answered him by fire and burnt up all the sacrifices and all the water.

Conclusion

The believer must be like Jabez who made some choices. The believers must be willing to step out on God's Word and ask Him for what he wants. Jabez had several things against him, but he refused to allow things to hinder him. His name was against him. Sometimes the believer thinks that his race, his color, his financial status, or his education is against him. But God's Word tells him that if he is willing and obedient, that he could eat the good of the land (Isaiah 1:19). God's Word tells the believer that if he listens, observes, and obeys God's Word, the blessings will come upon him, overtake him and God would lift him above the nations on the earth (Deuteronomy 28:1). But it will never happen if believers puts roadblocks and limitations on God and His Word.

Lesson 9 • Fourth Week

Jabez came from a family that was noted for some dishonorable things, the Word says that he was more honorable than his brothers. He had faith to overcome that when he called on the God of Israel. The people worshipped many gods at that time, but Jabez made a choice to honor and call on the God of the heavens, the true and living God (1 Chronicles 4:10).

He was specific in his request to God. Paul said make your request known unto God. To deal with limitations the believer must be specific in his request (Philippians 4:6).

Questions

1. What are some of the things that limit what God will do for the believer?
2. How does a believer deal with the limitations?
3. How did israel limit the Holy One of Israel?
4. What happens when the limits are removed?

_____
_____
_____
_____
_____

Essential Thought

If you want an unlimited life; take the limits off of God.

Lesson 10 • First Week

THE STORY OF THE GOOD SAMARITAN

Background Reading
Leviticus 19:18; Proverbs 14:20; Matthew 19:19; 22:39; Mark 12:31; Luke 6:27; 10:29-37; Romans 12:10; Galatians 5:14

Devotional Reading
John 4:5-29

Central Verse

"And he must needs go through Samaria."
John 4:4, KJV

"He had to go through Samaria on the way."
John 4:4, NLT

Key Terms

Mixed Breed—Made up of or involving individuals or items of more than one kind: made up of or involving persons differing in race, national origin, religion, or class.

Samaritan—A native or inhabitant of Samaria: a person who is generous in helping those in distress.

Introduction

A Good Samaritan is one who voluntarily renders aid to another in distress although under no duty to do so. He is a person who has compassion, concern and is willing to do something about situations that is not their obligation. He is a person who will go out of his way to help someone in need, he will use his gifts, influence, and resources to help someone who needs help.

He is what the world calls a "good neighbor." Jesus expects every believer to be a good neighbor. He is the perfect example for believers to follow. He showed Himself to be a good neighbor, a friend and certainly a good Samaritan. The world would be a much better place to live in if it had more "Good Samaritans" walking around.

Jesus emphasized that the greatest commandment was that believers love one another, do good to those who have not done good to them. Love those who have not shown you any love. It's up to each believer to be an example of love to everyone he meets for it's with love and kindness that the believer can draw others.

Discussion

Jesus was an exceptionally good teacher of everything that He taught His disciples about. He and His disciples were walking along together as they normally did when He told them that He needed to go

Lesson 10 • First Week

to Samaria. Samaria was not a city that many Jews took time to go through. Normally they detoured around the city because the Jews and the Samaritans were not on good speaking terms.

The Samaritans were a group of people in the Bible who were mixed, half-Jews and half-Gentiles. They were the survivors of the Assyrians conquest and Babylonia. They survived through the time of Jesus until this present day. The Northern kingdom of Israel fell to the Assyrians who took many of the people of Israel as captives. But some stayed and intermarried with foreigners who was left there by the Assyrians.

According to Webster's Dictionary the Samaritan were first mentioned in the Bible in the Book of Ezra and Nehemiah in the 5th Century B.C. At that point, Babylon had given way to the Persian Empire. Nehemiah, a Jew, gained favor with the King and was able to return to Jerusalem to rebuild the walls. However, the Samaritans remained in the land, opposed the rebuilding efforts, and caused problems for Nehemiah and his fellow workers (Nehemiah 6:1-14). This was the beginning of the long-lasting hatred between the Jews and the Samaritans. There are many church members today who do not believe that different races of people ought to marry. They do like the people who lived on this earth during Jesus' time, they discriminate against those who are not of their race. But as many as are led by God, they are the Sons of God.

The parable of the Good Samaritan has many lessons that the believer can learn some positive things from. A Samaritan was traveling by and saw the man who was traveling from Jerusalem to Jericho, who had been attacked by robbers, stripped of his clothes, beat, and left for dead. A Priest saw him but passed by him on the other side, a Levite saw him, but he too passed by on the other side. But the Samaritan stopped, took pity on him, bandaged up his wounds, pouring in oil and wine. He put the man on his donkey and took him to an Inn and took care of him. The next day he took out two denarii and gave it to the Innkeeper and told him to look after him, and when he returned that he would reimburse him of any extra expenses that he may incur (Luke 10:30-35).

Jesus asked the question, which one was the neighbor? The man answered Jesus that the one who stopped and showed mercy. Jesus told him to do likewise. The word of the Lord says that if you see your brother in need and have this world's good and shut up your bowels of compassion, how dwells the love of God (1 John 3:17).

Anyone who does the will of God can be your neighbor, for a neighbor is a person who lives next door or near to a person referred to. He can live away from you a great distance, but if he's there for you in your time of need, he can be your neighbor.

Conclusion

What can the believer learn from the story of the Good Samaritan? The fact that God so loved the entire world that He sent Jesus to die for all who would receive Him. This lesson lets the believers know that God is of no respecter of persons, and they can see that Jesus cared about people of mixed blood. He loved those who were hated by others. This lesson lets the believers know that God is the God of all flesh, and He does not exclude any race of people for He is not influenced by the opinions of others. The believer must try to be like Jesus and remember that from one blood, God made all nations and His loves reaches all people. Others may criticize your actions and love toward others who are

Lesson 10 • First Week

not just like you, but it is the believer's responsibility to show love to everyone, just as Jesus showed love to the woman at the well.

The woman that Jesus met at the well, was an outcast to some people, but Jesus saw here as a neighbor. He said that he had a need to go through Samaria, but what He really was doing was going to see about the woman's need. Sometimes believers must go out of their way to meet the needs of someone else and become that good Samaritan. In the long run, he becomes the winner.

Questions

1. Why did Jesus tell the story of the "Good Samaritan"?
2. How can this story help you as an indivuial?
3. Why was there so much hatred between the Jews and the Samaritans?
4. What can you do to help the race situation?

_____
_____
_____
_____
_____
_____

Essential Thought

When you meet the needs of others; you really meet a need of your own.

Lesson 11 • Second Week

GOD'S PRESENCE AND PURPOSE IN YOUR LIFE

Background Reading
Psalm 23:5; 68:8; 114:7; Luke 15:10; Romans 9:11

Devotional Reading
1 Corinthians 1:20-31

Central Verse

"Glory and honor are in His presence; Strength and gladness are in His place."
1 Chronicles 16:27, KJV

"Honor and majesty surround Him; strength and joy fill His dwelling."
1 Chronicles 16:27, NLT

Key Terms

Quickening—To make or become alive: to begin growth and development.
Impactful—Having a forceful impact: producing a marked impression.
Blockers—Things or people who interrupt a process or flow.

Introduction

Every believer is called to the presence and purpose of God. God calls His believers to live in His presence under His authority and to His glory. The believer's purpose is the assignment God has designed for him to accomplish, or it is the problem on earth that he was sent to solve. He must start by using the tools that he already has in his hands. The word purpose means the reason something is done, created, or exists. As believers, they know that glorifying God is their ultimate purpose, but he must discover his personal purpose. The believer can find this purpose by fasting and praying, and by seeking God's Word and His will, and by developing that close relationship with his Father.

Discussion

The believer knows that God saved him, called him with a Holy calling, not according to works, but according to his own purpose and grace (2 Timothy 1:9). Salvation is by grace alone and is not based on any human efforts but based on God's gracious gift of His dear Son. Sometimes the question needs to be asked why are we alive? And then the believer needs to dig deeper into his purpose, which is the *why* behind his life and the calling which is the *how* it can be done as he lives out his life. Next, his *assignment* which is the *what* can be done as the believer surrenders his life to the leading of the Holy Spirit.

Lesson 11 • Second Week

God created each believer exactly how He wanted them and for a critically important purpose. He gave each believer unique abilities to serve Him and make an impact on the world. God does not want believers to be tricked into playing the comparison game and miss His specific purpose and calling that He has just for him. He does not want the believer feeling purposeless in his life. He wants him to allow Him to use him in ways that he may have never dreamed of and with a passion that he isn't aware he has.

God wants him to discover, dream, and define. The believer can go from that passion to an action plan armed with biblical principles and practical strategies. He can answer that higher call and move on to being a living legacy of love and a positive impact. People can imitate someone else, but the other person cannot be duplicated. Each believer must discover his own purpose and calling. Many are called but only a few are chosen, and you have been chosen to come into the presence of God.

When God calls a believer to His purpose and His presence, the believer becomes responsible to God and to man to live a life of impact and significance. God has blessed each one with gifts, talents, potentials, opportunities, and time to do what is necessary. God's plan and purpose for the believer's life is that he lives his life and meet and honor all His expectations. It is up to the believer to allow the quickening power of the Holy Spirit to cause him to rise and live the life that God intended for him.

Sometimes the believer will have to make decisions concerning his journey even when he knows that he is walking in his assignment. He must decide if the opposition is going to be an opportunity or an excuse. Is it worth the approval of God or man? Is what he's doing bringing glory to God? Is it helping to build the Kingdom of God? Is it being impactful to God's people? Is it building him up in God's presence? Knowing the answers to these questions is vital to determining what direction the believer's life will go and this can be very overwhelming.

Every believer should be so sure about his purpose that he can live free from anxiety and worry concerning his future. He must know that God is pleased and knows his name, loves him, is walking with him in the times of opposition. It is a time when the believer must know that he is living a life of fulfillment and fruitfulness. He must know that he's not just in God's face, but he is under God's divine influence, for he is a vessel of honor in God's kingdom, and he has true freedom and significance.

Conclusion

Each believer's purpose calls out to him asking him to discover and embrace his divine purpose and navigate through the obstructions of fear and self-reliance. While learning to listen to the Holy Spirit's gentle nudges. Stay in the scriptures gaining power from the examples of men and women who have gone on. Let the life lessons that are learned from their triumphs and failures guide your lives as you confront your purpose blockers. And, allow their stories to empower you to step into the assignment that God has given you. For in His presence there is fulness of joy.

Paul is a wonderful example of a believer whose passion was misdirected, but when God showed up, he was radically changed. God forgave Paul for his past sins and then used him to be one of the greatest missionaries in the history of the early Church. If God forgave Paul, He can and will forgive anyone and give them purpose. Paul was able to change the world because he allowed God to change him.

Just as Paul was just living and thinking he was doing what was right, God has many believers whose lives can be changed. God does not want the believer just living, not excelling in the area that He has called them. He wants His followers to excel, progressing fulfilling dreams and visions, living their life to the fullest, fulfilling their purpose in His presence.

Lesson 11 • Second Week

Questions

1. What is purpose?
2. How does a believer find his purpose?
3. How does a believer's purpose impact the lives of others?
4. What are some of the things that can block purpose from leading a believer into God's presence?

_____
_____
_____
_____
_____
_____

Essential Thought

God wants every believer to discover his calling and fulfill his purpose, but doing it in His presence.

Lesson 12 • Third Week

LEARNING TO INCREASE YOUR JOY

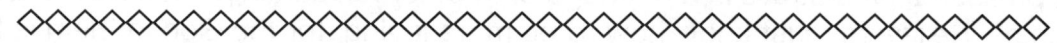

Background Reading
Psalm 126:5; Proverb 1:5-6; 9:9-10; 16:21-23; Zephaniah 3:17; John 15:11; 16:24

Devotional Reading
Habakkuk 3:17-19

Central Verse

"The meek also shall increase their joy in the Lord, and the poor among men shall rejoice in the Holy One of Israel."   Isaiah 29:19, KJV

"The humble will be filled with fresh joy from the Lord. The poor will rejoice in the Holy One of Israel."   Isaiah 29:19, NLT

Key Terms

Sustainer—A person or something that gives support or relief to.
Adamant—Unshakable or insistent especially in maintaining a position or opinion.
Navigate—To make one's way about, over, or through.
Encountering—A particular kind of meeting or experience with another person: a meeting face-to-face.

Introduction

Before you want to increase your joy, you must realize how important joy is in your life. There is a certain posture that a believer must get in so that his joy can increase. He must condition his mind and his spirit so that he can work on increasing his joy. Joy is a powerful emotion, and increasing it can remedy stress-related burnout. The joy of a believer should give them a feeling of immense pleasure and happiness. It should lift a believer out of feelings of despair and misery. Joy should cause a believer to be jubilant and joyful for contentment, and joy always helps to improve a person's mental and physical health. When a person feels joy, he feels great about himself; he feels confident, powerful, capable, lovable, and fulfilled.

Many believers allow life's problems to cause them to become fatigued, nervous, have headaches, or even experience feelings of depression. Increasing their joy will give them more strength, for the joy of the Lord is strength.

Discussion

It has been said that the emotion of joy can become confused with happiness, but there is a difference between happiness and joy. Happiness is an emotional reaction to what is happening around a person.

Lesson 12 • Third Week

Joy is based on internal things that are happening inside a person. It is said that "practice makes perfect." Well it's important that a believer make biblical joy a habit by encountering God every day and meditating on His word. Joy is a fundamental part of a believer's faith, so believers need to learn to reflect upon trials for this leads to moments of joy and peace. Wisdom is the mechanism between having trials and moving those trials into an enduring faith. As endurance, joy, and wisdom increase, the believer is further equipped to manage the trials that come into their lives. But during every trial, God will give the believer joy, and in a Christ-like manner, he will be able to navigate through his life.

The demands, pressures, and stress in a marriage or in other relationships can cause great strains on those relationships. Believers must know how to be more loving, for the God in them is love. This will increase the joy in the home, the workplace, church or wherever the believer may find himself. Choosing to be more grateful instead of allowing things to get him down, the believer will find himself having more joy in his life.

Some believers find themselves sad because they don't feel they are up to par in some areas. They strive but find that they fall so short of what they feel is God's expectations of them. They forget that salvation is only possible through grace. All their striving brings nothing but sorrow and accusations from the devil (Satan is an accuser of the Saints). This leaves the believer sad, depressed, down in his spirit and very discouraged. The believer must learn to let his joy in Christ increase on this journey of grace. Knowing that it is not of works, but it is the grace of God.

Without faith it is impossible to please God. Faith is the undercurrent of everything that a believer does when he is following Jesus. Without faith, the believer loses all that Christ died to give him while he lives here on earth.

True joy comes from God when the believer fully surrenders his heart to Him and embraces God's truth. He opens a space where joy will always be with him, but the believer must constantly seek to access that place of joy with God. Since God gives the believer joy, he must be adamant about taking a stand against the devil. He must resist the devil and cause him to flee, letting him know that he cannot have his joy.

The times that the believer feels low in joy, having feelings of discouragement, anxiety, and insecurity, he must take the time and stir up the joy that is within him. He can accomplish this by singing songs, reading praise scriptures and praying in the spirit. The book of Psalm has many psalms that will give the believers a great pick-up, if we take time and read some of them.

Conclusion

Jesus has a way of offering the believer an everlasting joy that will hold him up no matter what happens to come his way. First the believer must hold fast to the profession of his faith; he must choose to have joy like a river springing up like everlasting life. Yes, the believer faces many difficult seasons in his life. Yet he has the power that comes from the Holy Spirit to remind himself that Jesus came early one morning and was laid in a manger. But He didn't stay there, He went on to the cross where He gave His life which brought joy to the world.

Joy to the world, our Lord has come, let earth receive her King, let every heart proclaim that joyful sound, for Jesus is here to save His people from their sins. For God so loved the world that He gave

Lesson 12 • Third Week

His only begotten Son. God cares about every soul and does not want any to perish, but to have everlasting life. God not only cares but He is a sustainer and will always come to the rescue of His children.

Questions

1. How important is joy in the life of a believer?
2. What can the believer do to increase his joy?
3. What part does the Holy Spirit have in increasing the believer's joy?
4. The more joy a believer has does what to him?

_____
_____
_____
_____
_____

Essential Thought

The believer can have houses, land, jewels, or money; but if he doesn't have God in his life, he has nothing.

Lesson 13 • Fourth Week

JOY KILLERS

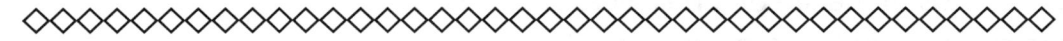

Background Reading
Psalm 33:17; Jeremiah 33:9; Luke 6:23; John 10:10; Acts 20:24; Philippians 3:7, James 1:1-4;

Devotional Reading
1 Samuel 4:5-11

Central Verse

"My brethren, count it all joy when ye fall into divers' temptation."
James 1:2, KJV

"Dear brothers and sisters, when troubles of any kind come your way, consider it an opportunity for great joy."
James 1:2, NLT

Key Terms

Word—A sound or combination of sounds that has meaning and is spoken by a human being: a written or printed letter or letters standing for a spoken word.
Wrath—Violent anger: punishment for sin or crime.

Introduction

While studying the importance of joy, the believers must remember that the enemy of their soul is not happy when their joy is full. When they find themselves falling into temptations but can yet rejoice in the God of their salvation. So, prepare yourself, for the enemy that comes to steal kill and to destroy. The joy killers are always lurking around trying to bring defeat into the believer's heart. The believer's hope and confidence must always be in Jesus Christ his Lord and Savior. When the enemy or the joy killers come in like a flood, the Spirit of the Lord Jesus will lift up a standard against the enemy (Isaiah 59:19).

Discussion

The song says, "This joy I have the world didn't give it to me, the world didn't give it and the world can't take it away." But the believers are not ignorant concerning the deceitfulness of the devil. He knows that there are several joy killers around, seeking whoever they can deceive. Some of the joy killers include unresolved conflict, comparison, complaining, pride and anxiety. All five of these can be deadly to the joy that is in the believer's lives.

The word of the Lord tells the believer's not to let the sun go down on their wrath, (Be angry, and sin not: let not the sun go down on your wrath) Ephesians 4:26. Do not allow unresolved conflicts to fester in your spirit. God's word lets believers know that if they do not deal with unresolved issues, they will allow anger to turn them into "mockers" and fools. The believers must ask their father for help so they can be healed by letting go of the anger and the issues and become transformed into peacemakers. Embrace the wisdom of God and receive the promises of peace within themselves as well as peace with others.

Pride cannot go with a believer to the next level of his commitment to God for pride is a joy killer. Pride cannot promote a believer because it will impede his growth. The believer must allow God to lead him into paths of righteousness and through the storms of life, and pride won't allow that. God is with the believer through every season of his life for He never leaves nor forsakes His children. He will be with them as they go through. But they must never focus on the waves nor the fire. They must maintain a focus on God and His mighty wonder working power. A haughty spirit goes before a fall.

The next joy killer is Comparison or envy. Theodore Roosevelt, the 26th President of the United States of America, said, "Comparison is the thief of joy". It is important to remember that each believer has been given different gifts and each believer is expected to give God his absolute best. His best may not be like someone else's best, but when he gives his best, that's all he can do. God gives each believer the grace that he needs, not what someone else needs. In 2 Corinthians 10:12 Paul gives a clear understanding when he says, "For we dare not class ourselves or compare ourselves with those who commend themselves. But they, measuring themselves by themselves, and comparing among themselves, are not wise." Paul was one of the Apostles who dealt with envy and comparison. He refused to allow any of the words or actions of the other disciples affect his effectiveness nor his work in the ministry stop him. God wants each believer to have joy in his walk with Him in implementing their assignment.

Pride is a powerful joy killer. It is so bad that God says He hates a proud look. John said all that is in the world is the lust of the eye, the lust of the flesh and the pride of life. So, pride is a powerful weapon that Satan uses to kill the believer's joy. The believer can choose to be humble, or he can choose to be prideful. He can choose to let the spirit of heaviness weigh him down or he can choose to let God lift every burden. He can choose to worship God or choose to worship the weights and the bondages of his past. A haughty spirit goes before a fall and blocks the joy bells that want to ring in the believer's soul. Thank God believers don't have to allow the joy killers to kill their confidence in God but can redirect their focus on God and not on the weight of this world. The believer must remember that this is Jesus's world, and He has already died for its sins, so they don't have to.

The next joy killer is complaining. The children of Israel were so blessed by God in so many ways, but they complained to Moses about some of everything. God blesses His children and supplies every need, but some believers allow the spirit of murmuring and complaining to come from them every day. How can a person have joy when all he does is complain every day? He has no time to praise and rejoice because he is so busy complaining. Paul advised the believer to do everything without complaining. He told them to stop grumbling and disputing that they may be blameless and innocent children of God. God has called the believers to a higher calling which includes counting all things as joy, not complaining.

Conclusion

The next joy killer in this lesson is Anxiety. This is a big joy killer because anxiety creeps into the heart of a believer and into the mind where the peace of God should always be. The word tells the believer

Lesson 13 • Fourth Week

not to be anxious about anything, but with prayer and supplication with thanksgiving let their request be made known to God. And the peace of God which surpasses all understanding, will guard your hearts and minds in Christ Jesus (Philippians 4:6-7). Believers, you must not allow yourself to become ignorant concerning the devices of Satan. He's out to get you, He will steal everything that is good about you and leave you as a fallen Saint of God. Satan knows if you have joy, you can laugh, and laughter does good like medicine. So, don't let the devil ride, if you let him ride, he'll want to drive. Do not let him kill your joy, hold on to your joy.

Questions

1. Why does the enemy want to steal your joy?
2. What are some of the joy killers?
3. How can the believer prevent the steal?
4. Why are joy killer's dangerous to the body of Christ?

_____

_____

_____

_____

_____

_____

Essential Thought

Where there's joy there is laughter, and laughter is like medicine; and where there is medicine there is healing of body, mind, and spirit.

NOTES

The Presiding Bishop, Chairman of the Publishing Board, General Supervisor of the Department of Women, Contributing Writers, and the entire Prayer & Bible Band Topics Editorial Staff would like to thank you for your continued support.

Bishop J. Drew Sheard
Presiding Bishop

Bishop Uleses C. Henderson, Jr.
Chairman, Publishing Board

Mother Barbara McCoo Lewis
*General Supervisor,
Department of Women*

Supervisor Lee Etta Van Zandt
Contributing Writer

Supervisor Francis S. Curtis
Contributing Writer

Elder Joseph W. Gill
Contributing Writer

1-877-746-8578 | WWW.COGICPUBLISHINGHOUSE.NET

CHURCH OF GOD IN CHRIST DOCTRINE

THE BIBLE
We believe that the Bible is the Word of God and contains one harmonious and sufficiently complete system of doctrine. We believe in the full inspiration of the Word of God. We hold the Word of God to be the only authority in all matters and assert that no doctrine can be true or essential, if it does not find a place in this Word.

THE FATHER
We believe in God, the Father Almighty, the Author and Creator of all things. The Old Testament reveals God in diverse manners, by manifesting His nature, character, and dominions. The Gospels in the New Testament give us knowledge of God the "Father" or "My Father", showing the relationship of God to Jesus as Father, or representing Him as the Father in the Godhead, and Jesus Himself that Son (John 15:8, 14:20). Jesus also gives God the distinction of "Fatherhood" to all believers when He explains God in the light of "Your Father in Heaven" (Matthew 6:8).

THE SON
We believe that Jesus Christ is the Son of God, the Second person in the Godhead of the Trinity or Triune Godhead. We believe that Jesus was and is eternal in His person and nature as the Son of God who was with God in the beginning of creation (John 1:1). We believe that Jesus Christ was born of a virgin called Mary according to the Scripture (Matthew 1:18), thus giving rise to our fundamental belief in the Virgin Birth and to all of the miraculous events surrounding the phenomenon (Matthew 1:18–25). We believe that Jesus Christ became the "suffering servant" to man; this suffering servant came seeking to redeem man from sin and to reconcile him back to God, his Father (Romans 5:10). We believe that Jesus Christ is standing now as mediator between God and man (I Timothy 2:5)

THE HOLY GHOST
We believe the Holy Ghost or Holy Spirit is the third person of the Trinity, proceeds from the Father and the Son, is of the same substance, equal to power and glory, and is together with the Father and the Son, to be believed in, obeyed, and worshipped. The Holy Ghost is a gift bestowed upon the believer for the purpose of equipping and empowering the believer, making him a more effective witness for service in the world. He teaches and guides one into all truth (John 16:13; Acts 1:8, 8:39).

THE BAPTISM OF THE HOLY GHOST
We believe that the Baptism of the Holy Ghost is an experience subsequent to conversion and sanctification and that tongue–speaking is the consequence of the baptism in the Holy Ghost with the manifestations of the fruit of the spirit (Galatians 5:22–23; Acts 10:46, 19:1–6). We believe that we are not baptized with the Holy Ghost in order to be saved but that we are baptized with the Holy Ghost because we are saved. (Acts 19:1–6; John 3:5). When one receives a baptismal Holy Ghost experience, we believe one will speak with a tongue unknown to oneself according to the sovereign will of Christ. To be filled with the Spirit means to be Spirit controlled as expressed by Paul in Ephesians 5:18–19. Since the charismatic demonstrations were necessary to help the early church to be successful in implementing the command of Christ, we therefore, believe that a Holy Ghost experience is mandatory for all men today.

MAN
We believe that man was created Holy by God, composed of body, soul, and spirit. We believe that man, by nature, is sinful and unholy. Being born in sin, he needs to be born again, sanctified and cleansed from all sins by the blood of Jesus. We believe that man is saved by confessing and forsaking his sins, and believing on the Lord Jesus Christ, and that having become a child of God, by being born again and adopted into the family of God, he may, and should, claim the inheritance of the sons of God, namely the baptism of the Holy Ghost.

SIN
Sin, the Bible teaches, began in the angelic world (Ezekiel 28:11–19; Isaiah 14:12–20), and is transmitted into the blood of the human race through disobedience and deception motivated by unbelief (I Timothy 2:14). Adam's sin, committed by eating of the forbidden fruit from the tree of knowledge of good and evil, carried with it permanent pollution or depraved human nature to all his descendants. This is called "original sin." Sin can now be defined as a volitional transgression against God and a lack of conformity to the will of God. We, therefore, conclude that man by nature, is sinful and that he has fallen from a glorious and righteous state from which he was created, and has become unrighteous and unholy. Man, therefore, must be restored to his state of holiness from which he has fallen by being born again (John 3:7).

SALVATION
Salvation deals with the application of the work of redemption to the sinner and with his restoration to divine favor and communion with God. This redemptive operation of the Holy Ghost upon sinners is brought about by repentance toward God and faith toward our Lord Jesus Christ which brings conversion, Faith, Justification Regeneration, Sanctification, and the Baptism of the Holy Ghost. Repentance is the work of God, which results in a change of mind in respect to man's relationship to God. (Matthew 3:1–2, 4:17; Acts 20:21). Faith is a certain conviction wrought in the heart by the Holy Spirit, as to the truth of the Gospel and a heart trust in the promises of God in Christ (Romans 1:17, 3:28; Matthew 9:22; Acts 26:18). Conversion is that act of God whereby He causes the regenerated sinner, in his conscious life, to turn to Him in repentance and faith (II Kings 5:15; II Chronicles 33:12–13; Luke 19:8–9; Acts 8:30). Regeneration is that act of God by which the principle of the new life is implanted in man, and the governing disposition of soul is made holy and the first holy exercise of this new disposition is secured. Sanctification is that gracious and continuous operation of the Holy Ghost, by which He delivers the justified sinner from the pollution of sin, renews his whole nature in the image of God and enables him to perform good works (Romans 6:4, 5:6; Colossians 2:12, 3:1).

ANGELS
The Bible uses the term "angel" (a heavenly body) clearly and primarily to denote messengers or ambassadors of God with such Scripture references as Revelations 4:5, which indicates their duty in heaven to praise God (Psalm 103:20), to do God's will (Matthew 18:10) and to behold His face. But since heaven must come down to earth, they also have a mission to earth. The Bible indicates that they accompanied God in the Creation, and also that they will accompany Christ in His return in Glory.

DEMONS
Demons denote unclean or evil spirits; they are sometimes called devils or demonic beings. They are evil spirits, belonging to the unseen or spiritual realm, embodied in human beings. The Old Testament refers to the prince of demons, sometimes called Satan (Adversary) or Devil, as having power and wisdom, taking the habitation of other forms such as the serpent (Genesis 3:1). The New Testament speaks of the Devil as Tempter (Matthew 4:3) and it goes on to tell the works of Satan, The Devil, and Demons as combating righteousness and good in any form, proving to be an adversary to the saints. Their chief power is exercised to destroy the mission of Jesus Christ. It can well be said that the Christian Church believes in Demons, Satan, and Devils. We believe in their power and purpose. We believe they can be subdued and conquered as in the commandment to the believer by Jesus. " In my name they shall cast out devils;" and the work of the Devil and to resist him and then he will flee (WITHDRAW) from you. (Mark 16:17).

THE CHURCH
The Church forms a spiritual unity of which Christ is the divine head. It is animated by one Spirit, the Spirit of Christ. It professes one faith, shares one hope, and serves one King. It is the citadel of the truth and God's agency for communicating to believers all spiritual blessings. The Church then is the object of our faith rather than of knowledge. The name of our Church, "CHURCH OF GOD IN CHRIST" is supported by I Thessalonians 2:14 and other passages in the Pauline Epistles. The word "CHURCH" or "EKKLESIA" was first applied to the Christian society by Jesus Christ in Matthew 16:18, the occasion being that of his benediction of Peter at Caesarea Philippi.

THE SECOND COMING OF CHRIST
We believe in the second coming of Christ; that He shall come from heaven to earth, personally, bodily, visibly (Acts 1:11; Titus 2:11–13; Matthew 16:27; 24:30; 25:30; Luke 21:27, John 1:14, 17, Titus 2:11) and that the Church, the bride, will be caught up to meet Him in the air (I Thessalonians 4:16–17). We admonish all who have this hope to purify themselves as He is pure.

DIVINE HEALING
The Church Of God In Christ believes in and practices Divine Healing. It is a commandment of Jesus to the Apostles (Mark 16:18). Jesus affirms His teachings on healing by explaining to His disciples, who were to be Apostles, that healing the afflicted is by faith (Luke 9:40–41). Therefore, we believe that healing by faith in God has scriptural support and ordained authority. St. James' writings in his epistle encourage Elders to pray for the sick, lay hands upon them and to anoint them with oil, and that prayers with faith shall heal the sick and the Lord shall raise them up. Healing is still practiced widely and frequently in the Church Of God In Christ, and testimonies of healing in our Church testify to this fact.

MIRACLES
The Church Of God In Christ believes that miracles occur to convince men that the Bible is God's Word. A miracle can be defined as an extraordinary visible act of Divine power, wrought by the efficient agency of the will of God, which has as its final cause the vindication of the righteousness of God's Word. We believe that the works of God, which were performed during the beginnings of Christianity, do and will occur even today where God is preached, Faith in Christ is exercised, The Holy Ghost is active, and the Gospel is promulgated in the truth (Acts 5:15, 6:8, 9:40; Luke 4:36, 5:5–6, 7:14–15; Mark 14:15).

THE ORDINANCES OF THE CHURCH
It is generally admitted that for an ordinance to be valid, it must have been instituted by Christ. When we speak of ordinances of the Church, we are speaking of those instituted by Christ, in which by sensible signs the grace of God in Christ, and the benefits of the covenant of grace are represented, sealed, and applied to believers, and these in turn give expression to their faith and allegiance to God. The Church Of God In Christ recognizes three ordinances as having been instituted by Christ Himself and therefore, binding upon the Church practice.

A. THE LORD'S SUPPER (HOLY COMMUNION)
The Lord's Supper symbolizes the Lord's death and suffering for the benefit and in the place of His people. It also symbolizes the believer's participation in the crucified Christ. It represents not only the death of Christ as the object of faith which unites the believers to Christ, but also the effect of this act as the giving of life, strength, and joy to the soul. The communicant by faith enters into a special spiritual union of his soul with the glorified Christ.

B. FEET WASHING
Feet Washing is practiced and recognized as an ordinance in our Church because Christ, by His example, showed that humility characterized greatness in the Kingdom of God, and that service, rendered to others gave evidence that humility, motivated by love, exists. These services are held subsequent to the Lord's Supper; however, its regularity is left to the discretion of the Pastor in charge.

C. WATER BAPTISM
We believe that Water Baptism is necessary as instructed by Christ in John 3:5, "UNLESS MAN BE BORN AGAIN OF WATER AND OF THE SPIRIT."

However, we do not believe that water baptism alone is a means of salvation, but is an outward demonstration that one has already had a conversion experience and has accepted Christ as his personal Savior. As Pentecostals, we practice immersion in preference to "SPRINKLING", because immersion corresponds more closely to the death, burial, and resurrection of our Lord (Colossians 2:12). It also symbolizes regeneration and purification more than any other mode. Therefore, we practice immersion as our mode of Baptism. We believe that we should use the Baptismal Formula given us by Christ for all "...IN THE NAME OF THE FATHER, AND OF THE SON, AND OF THE HOLY GHOST." (Matthew 28:19)

The Church Of God In Christ Statement Of Faith

We believe the Bible to be the inspired and only infallible written Word of God.
We believe that there is only One God, eternally existent in three persons: God the Father, God the Son, and God the Holy Spirit.
We believe in the blessed Hope, which is the rapture of the Church of God, which is in Christ, at His return.
We believe that the only means of being cleansed from sin is through repentance and faith in the precious Blood of Jesus Christ.
We believe that regeneration by the Holy Ghost is absolutely essential for personal salvation.
We believe that the redemptive work of Christ on the Cross provides healing for the human body in answer to believing prayer.
We believe that the Baptism of the Holy Spirit, according to Acts 2:4, is given to believers who ask for it.
We believe in the sanctifying power of the Holy Spirit, by whose indwelling the Christian is enabled to live a holy and separated life in this present world.